D1273554

HAUNTED
BATTLEFIELDS

LITTLE BIGHORN

HISTORY AND LEGEND
BY
EARLE RICE JR.

PURPLE TOAD
PUBLISHING

HAUNTED
BATTLEFIELDS

ANTIETAM by Russell Roberts
GETTYSBURG by Russell Roberts
LITTLE BIGHORN by Earle Rice Jr.
VERDUN by Earle Rice Jr.

PUBLISHER'S NOTE
The data in this book has been researched in depth, and to the best of our knowledge is factual. Although every measure is taken to give an accurate account, Purple Toad Publishing makes no warranty of the accuracy of the information and is not liable for damages caused by inaccuracies.

ABOUT THE AUTHOR
Earle Rice Jr. is a former senior design engineer and technical writer in the aerospace, electronic-defense, and nuclear industries. He has devoted full time to his writing since 1993 and is the author of more than seventy published books. Earle is listed in **Who's Who in America** and is a member of the Society of Children's Book Writers and Illustrators, the League of World War I Aviation Historians, the Air Force Association, and the Disabled American Veterans.

Printing 1 2 3 4 5 6 7 8 9

Publisher's Cataloging-in-Publication Data
Rice Jr., Earle
  Little Bighorn / Earle Rice, Jr..
    p. cm.
Includes bibliographic references.
ISBN 9781624691188
1. Little Bighorn, Battle of the, Mont., 1876—Juvenile literature. 2. Indians of North America—Wars—Juvenile literature. 3. Custer, George A. (George Armstrong), 1839-1876--Juvenile literature. 4. Sitting Bull, 1831-1890—Juvenile literature. I. Series: Haunted battlefields.
  E83.876
  973.82092

Library of Congress Control Number: 2014945190

ebook ISBN: 9781624691195

CONTENTS

CHAPTER

ONE

"WE SHALL FIGHT AS BRAVE MEN FIGHT"

Late one night in 1980, Mardell Plainfeather and her daughter Lorena ventured out into the darkness along the Little Bighorn River. Mardell was then a park ranger at the Custer Battlefield National Monument. She and Lorena were members of the Crow Indian Tribe. They faithfully held to the old practices of their people.

On this night, the two women were on their way to the family sweat lodge. The lodge was nestled discreetly in the thick timber across the river from the battlefield. Mardell wanted to make sure the fire was out in the lodge before retiring. Neither mother nor daughter was prepared for what they were about to see.

"I don't make a habit of going out in the dark by myself, but I was in my car so I wasn't scared or anything," Mardell said later. "I had never had any supernatural experiences before and I was certainly not prepared for one, but when I saw them, it didn't scare me at all."[1]

For whatever reason, her eyes were drawn upward toward the bluffs on the far side of the river. There, silhouetted against a moonlit sky, she saw two Indian warriors sitting on their horses.

★ ★ ★ ★ ★ ★ ★ ★ ★ ★ ★ ★ ★ ★ ★ ★ ★

A vision of two Indian warriors silhouetted against a moonlit sky appeared to park ranger Mardell Plainfeather late one night in 1980. They were sitting on their horses atop a bluff at the Custer Battlefield National Monument. No horses are allowed there, and she found no trace of their presence the next day.

They were dressed for war, with painted faces and feathers laid low in their hair. One wore braids. Both warriors carried shields, and one brandished a bow. They were phantom visitors from the spirit world, within the confines of the fenced-in battlefield. One spirit raised himself in his saddle and peered down directly at Mardell. In the darkness, she could not tell whether the warriors were Crow, Sioux, or Cheyenne.

"Even if they were Sioux or Cheyenne spirits, they didn't mean me any harm at all," she said with certainty. "Perhaps they were just trying to tell me that I was doing a good job of interpreting the battle story to our visitors. Perhaps they were just trying to tell me that they were happy that a Native American, no matter what tribe, was finally telling their side of the story. Maybe their spirits were restless. . . ."[2]

The next day, Mardell went up to the bluff and examined the grounds. She found no traces that horses or warriors had been there. Significantly, no one is allowed on the battlefield after dark, and horses are not allowed there at any time. Mardell said prayers for the dead of the Little Bighorn and left them offerings of sage and tobacco. She never saw the spirit warriors again.

Mardell's sighting of two warrior spirits in 1980 is but one of the many ghostly encounters that have been reported over the years at the Custer battleground. The site of one of the worst defeats in U.S. military history has since acquired a reputation as one of the most haunted places in America.

Otherworldly experiences associated with Lieutenant Colonel George Armstrong Custer and his so-called Last Stand at the Little Bighorn began as early as May 17, 1876. On that day, he marched his column of the U.S. Seventh Cavalry out of Fort Abraham Lincoln, near present-day Bismarck, North Dakota, and headed west. The regimental band played "The Girl He Left Behind," as the troopers ascended a slope outside the fort.

Custer's wife, Elizabeth, or "Libbie," watched the column leave through a rising, sun-warmed morning mist. "A mirage appeared," Libbie wrote later, "which took up about half of the line of cavalry, and thenceforth for a little distance it marched, equally plain to the sight on the earth and in the sky."[3] To her and others who saw the illusion, it looked as though the Seventh Cavalry was marching straight up into the heavens to meet its predetermined fate.

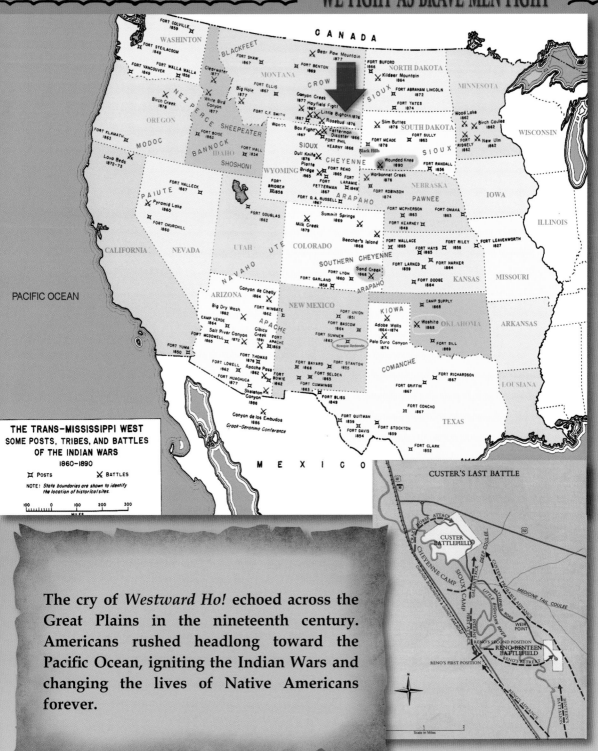

THE TRANS-MISSISSIPPI WEST
SOME POSTS, TRIBES, AND BATTLES
OF THE INDIAN WARS
1860-1890

⊨ POSTS   ✕ BATTLES

NOTE: *State boundaries are shown to identify the location of historical sites.*

100 0 100 200 300
MILES

CUSTER'S LAST BATTLE

The cry of *Westward Ho!* echoed across the Great Plains in the nineteenth century. Americans rushed headlong toward the Pacific Ocean, igniting the Indian Wars and changing the lives of Native Americans forever.

Elizabeth "Libbie" Bacon Custer and Brigadier General George Armstrong Custer posed for this photograph shortly after their marriage on February 9, 1864.

Scientifically, Libbie and others had viewed a mirage known as a superior image. It was formed by light rays from the warm upper air reflecting off the colder air from the valley below to create a duplicate image above the heads of the troopers. Whether it foretold the future of Custer's ill-fated regiment is pure speculation. But to Libbie Custer, who feared for the safety of her husband and his regiment, "the future of the heroic band seemed to be revealed."[4] At the very least, the mirage deserves a place among the endless myths surrounding Custer's role in the Sioux Indian Wars of 1876.

In 1874, Custer led an expedition into the Black Hills, a sacred Indian hunting ground, to investigate rumors of gold in the area. He soon confirmed the discovery of gold on French Creek, near what is now Custer, South Dakota. His news triggered the Black Hills Gold Rush. Earlier treaties between the Indians and the U.S. government had prohibited white settlement in the unceded Dakota Territory. The sudden influx of white gold-seekers and settlers violated treaty agreements.

Angered and saddened by the white man's betrayal, Sitting Bull, the spiritual leader of the Sioux, said, "We have been deceived by the white people. The Black Hills country was set aside for us by the Government."[5] Accordingly, the Sioux had made the Black Hills their home. Now, with the discovery of gold, the white man

Sitting Bull, a Hunkpapa Lakota chief and holy man, became one of the most photographed people of the late 19th century after his victory over Custer at the Little Bighorn.

Chiefs Gall (left), Sitting Bull, and Crazy Horse cast in bronze. Sitting Bull's vision of victory inspired the triumph of his followers at the Little Bighorn. Gall led an early attack, and Crazy Horse led the charge that killed Custer.

and his soldiers were invading their home. Understandably, the Sioux feared for their homes and families.

"[I]f the Government lets loose an army upon us to kill without mercy," Sitting Bull continued, "we shall fight as brave men fight. We shall meet our enemies and honorably defeat them, or we shall all of us die in disgrace."[6] Many angry Sioux and Cheyenne left their reservations and joined Sitting Bull and the Oglala war leader Crazy Horse in Montana.

George Armstrong Custer was one of history's rare characters who become legends in their own time. He was born in New Rumley, Ohio, on December 5, 1839. From childhood's hour, he aspired to greatness. His quest for glory began on a low note when he graduated last in his class at West Point in 1861. Only the outbreak of the Civil War saved him from sure expulsion from the U.S. Military Academy.

Despite his uninspiring beginning, Custer hit his stride as a cavalry commander in the Union Army during the Civil War. Exercising uncommon courage and daring, he quickly rose from second lieutenant to the brevet rank of brigadier general of volunteers at the age of 23. Custer's vigorous pursuit of Confederate General Robert E. Lee in retreat from Richmond hastened Lee's surrender in 1865.

After the Civil War, Custer's rank reverted to his earlier rank of captain. In 1866, he was transferred to the Western Frontier. He quickly won fame as an Indian fighter and was promoted to lieutenant colonel. Always ambitious, Custer looked forward to earning the permanent rank of general, with an eye on the presidency of the United States.

In 1867, Custer looked back on his life and assessed his early aspirations. "In years long numbered with the past, when I was merging upon manhood," he stated, "my every thought was ambitious—not to be wealthy, not to be learned, but to be great. I desired to link my name with acts and men, and in such manner as to be a mark of honor, not only to the present but to future generations."[7] Custer's pursuit of greatness ended on a low note, as it had begun, nine years later at Montana's Little Bighorn River—but his story lives on.

Custer the cadet at West Point

CHAPTER

TWO

SOLDIERS FALLING INTO CAMP

On November 3, 1875, President Ulysses S. Grant paced the floor of his White House office, pondering the pesky "Indian question." He had called his top government and military advisers to a secret meeting to discuss the problem. It was decision time.

After the Treaty of Laramie in 1868, most of the Northern Plains Indians had retired to live peacefully on the Great Sioux Reservation. The reservation occupied most of what is now South Dakota. Reservation Indians included a few northern Cheyenne, Arapaho, and Dakota (eastern Sioux), but most were Lakota (western Sioux). The Lakota consisted of seven subtribes or bands: Oglala, Minneconjou, Brulé, Hunkpapa, Sans Arcs, Blackfeet, and Two Kettles.

Some three thousand Indians—about four hundred Cheyenne and a mix of Lakota—decided to live independently off the reservation. The government called them *nontreaty* Indians. Except for a few minor clashes among the "nontreaties," most of the Indians had remained peaceful until the mid-1870s. But after the discovery

★ ★ ★ ★ ★ ★ ★ ★ ★ ★ ★ ★ ★ ★ ★ ★ ★

Ulysses S. Grant was highly regarded by his peers as a perceptive and effective Civil War general. Many of his countrymen attribute his poor performance as a politician to his naïve confidence in unworthy colleagues and associates.

After the Battle of the Little Bighorn, the U.S. Army subdued the Northern Cheyenne in 1877 and forced them to relocate to the reservation at Fort Reno with the Southern Cheyenne.

of gold in the Black Hills, hostile encounters between Indians and white gold-seekers and settlers began to occur with alarming frequency.

President Grant paused in front of the white mantelpiece in his White House office and peered into the flames of a warming winter fire. Should he send the army against trespassing whites to enforce the law? Or should he use the army against law-abiding Indians to seize their lands and claim them as spoils of war? As he struggled with the answer to the troubling Indian question, he glanced upward at the portrait of Abraham Lincoln above the mantel. *What would Lincoln do?* he wondered.

Grant considered the Indians to be obstacles in the path of America's Manifest Destiny—its inherent right to expand its boundaries west to the Pacific Ocean. He opted to make war. He directed General Philip H. Sheridan to prepare for a campaign against the Indians. Secretary of Interior Zachariah Chandler notified the commissioner of Indian Affairs to instruct the nontreaty Indians to "remove to a reservation before the 31st of January next." If they failed to do so, they would "be reported to the War Department as hostile Indians," and a military force would "be sent to compel them to obey the orders of the Indian Office."[1]

None of the nontreaty Indians reported to a reservation by the January deadline, but General Sheridan was ready with a plan. It called for a winter campaign against the Indians, with three columns converging from different directions.

On March 1, 1876, General George Crook left Fort Fetterman, in Wyoming Territory, and marched north with a column of 900 men. In the meantime, the other two columns were to organize under General Alfred H. Terry in the Department of Dakota. One column, led by Colonel John Gibbon, would then trek

Civil war days—Generals Wesley Merritt (left), Philip Sheridan, George Crook, James William Forsyth, and George Armstrong Custer confer.

east out of Montana, while the other column under Lieutenant Colonel George A. Custer would march west from Fort Abraham Lincoln.

In practice, General Sheridan's plan quickly faltered. Of the two Dakota columns, only Gibbon's column marched. Heavy snows postponed Custer's departure. Meanwhile, General Crook's column of some 900 infantry and cavalry moved northward, battling snow and icy winds. On the morning of March 17, he sent 300 cavalry under Colonel Joseph J. Reynolds to attack an Indian camp of 105 lodges at the Powder River.

The Indians, Cheyenne and Oglalas, were unaware of the cavalry's approach until the crack of the first bullet. Then chaos erupted. Wooden Leg, a Cheyenne warrior, later recalled: "Women screamed. Children cried for their mothers. Old people tottered and hobbled away to get out of reach of the bullets singing among the lodges. Braves seized whatever weapons they had and tried to meet the attack."[2]

On March 17, 1876, a cavalry troop led by Colonel Joseph J. Reynolds charged into an Indian camp of 105 lodges in the Powder River valley. The surprised Oglalas and Cheyennes fled to the bordering bluffs, regrouped, counterattacked, and forced the troopers to withdraw.

After the Battle of Powder River, and three weeks of struggling against snow, ice, wind, and bitter cold, General George Crook elected to lead his worn-out detachment back to Fort Fetterman, Wyoming.

After their initial surprise, the Indians fought back fiercely. Reynolds ordered a retreat and pulled back timidly to rejoin Crook's main column. Angry, and running low on supplies, Crook returned to Fort Fetterman to regroup and resupply. The Indians struck camp and moved down the Powder to unite with Crazy Horse and the Oglalas.

The fight on Powder River convinced the Indians that the soldiers meant war. As battle fever spread among them, they united in a single village of about 450 lodges. Their numbers continued to swell as reservation Indians joined them for the spring hunting season. At the same time, General Sheridan recognized that a summer campaign was needed to bring the Indians under control. He rescheduled his three-column convergence campaign for late in the spring of 1876.

On May 17, General Terry moved west out of Fort Lincoln with a column of 925 troopers, including Custer's Seventh Cavalry. Terry was headed to a rendezvous with Gibbon on the Yellowstone River. Gibbon's force of 450 infantry and cavalry out of Forts Shaw and Ellis in Montana Territory was already at the river. General Crook's column, numbering more than a thousand troops, finally marched again out of Fort Fetterman on May 29. Crook was also bound for Yellowstone.

A group of Sioux gather for a Sun Dance, a sacred ceremony of many Plains Indians. The ceremony usually lasted for eight days and involved smoking, fasting, and the performance of humbling rites, some of them secret.

Early in June, the Indians held a religious ceremony known as a Sun Dance at their camp on the Rosebud River. Sitting Bull, "the leader of the entire Sioux nation,"[3] danced for a day and a half in the ceremony, then fell into a trance. When he finally came out of the trance, he spoke softly of a vision to his cousin Black Moon.

Black Moon rose and relayed Sitting Bull's vision to several thousand Cheyenne and Lakota gathered there: "He looked up and saw soldiers and some Indians on horseback coming down like grasshoppers, with their heads down and their hats falling off. They were falling right into our camp."[4] The Indians did not know it at the time, but the soldiers were already close at hand.

Sitting Bull was born somewhere along the Grand River in what is now South Dakota, probably in 1831. At the age of ten, he killed his first buffalo. His people named him *Tatanka-Iyotanka,* a Lakota name describing a buffalo bull sitting on its haunches. He inherited the chieftainship of the Hunkpapa band from his father, Jumping Bull.

The Lakota came to revere Sitting Bull as a *wichasha wakan,* a man who could reveal the will of the Great Mystery. He fought his first battle against the white man in 1863 and spent the rest of his life defending his people.

"I never taught my people to trust Americans," Sitting Bull said. "I have told them the truth—that the Americans are great liars. I have never dealt with the Americans. Why should I? The land belonged to my people."[5]

Near the end of his life, Sitting Bull had another vision like the one foretelling Custer's defeat: A meadowlark told him that his own people, the Lakota, would kill him.

On December 15, 1890, at the Standing Rock Indian Agency, Lakota police came to Sitting Bull's cabin to arrest him. Indian agents feared that he would join and inspire the Ghost Dance movement. Ghost Dancers advocated ridding the land of white people and restoring the Indian way of life. The police dragged Sitting Bull out of his cabin. A fight ensued. One of the Lakota policemen shot the old chief in the head and killed him.

Ghost dancers

CHAPTER

THREE

GREAT EXPECTATIONS

By June 16, 1876, Sitting Bull and his followers had moved their camp four times since his vision of soldiers falling into camp. Their lodges were now pitched along a tributary of the Little Bighorn called Sun Dance Creek. That evening, Lakota scouts rode into camp bringing news of the approach of Three Stars and his soldiers. Three Stars was their name for General Crook. Tribal leaders gathered in the council lodge. Crazy Horse rose to speak.

"It is time to put an end to the white man in our land," he said. "It is time to finish this thing. I will ride against Three Stars. Those who wish can come with me."[1] More than a thousand warriors joined him at the edge of camp, and they rode out to meet Crook and a roughly equal number of his blue-coated soldiers.

On the morning of June 17, Crook called a halt to his column at a broad, rolling stretch of grassland along the Rosebud River. He sent his Crow scouts ahead to look for signs of the Lakota and Cheyenne. Soon, the sound of gunfire echoed from beyond a nearby ridge. The Crow scouts had run into the first Lakota warriors to arrive on scene.

★ ★ ★ ★ ★ ★ ★ ★ ★ ★ ★ ★ ★ ★ ★ ★ ★

On June 17, 1876, more than a thousand Sioux and Cheyenne warriors clashed with an equal number of U.S. cavalry under General George Crook at the Rosebud River in southeastern Montana. The Indians fought fiercely and Crook was again forced to withdraw.

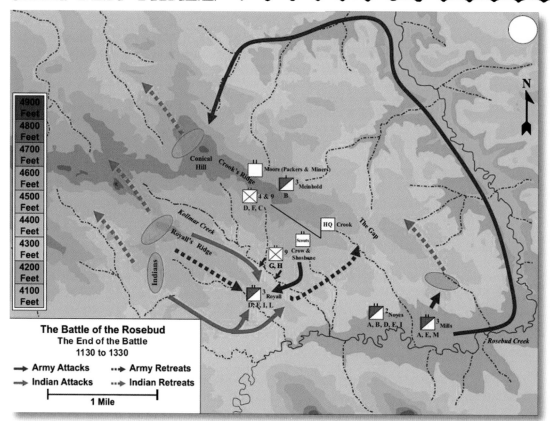

The Battle of the Rosebud
The End of the Battle
1130 to 1330

→ Army Attacks   ⋯➤ Army Retreats
→ Indian Attacks   ⋯➤ Indian Retreats

⊢――――――――――⊣
1 Mile

Sioux and Cheyenne warriors demonstrated their riding abilities at the Battle of the Rosebud and proved that as cavalry they were second to none.

"Hokahe!" Crazy Horse yelled. "Come on! Do not be afraid! It is a good day to die!"[2] And the Battle of the Rosebud began.

A bloody, brutal battle between Indians and white men ensued for the next six hours. The cavalrymen expected the Indians to cut and run once the column's full force was brought to bear on them, but they did not.

"The Indians proved then and there that they were the best cavalry soldiers on earth," Captain Anson Mills wrote later. "In charging up toward us they exposed little of their person, hanging on with one arm around the neck and one leg over the horse, firing and lancing from underneath the horse's necks, so that there was no part of the Indian at which to aim."[3]

To Crook's besieged troopers it seemed as if Crazy Horse's attackers were coming at them from every direction. "The Indians came not in a line but in flocks or herds like the buffalo," Mills recalled, "and they piled in upon us."[4] The fighting

continued with a fury, each side giving no quarter, until the Indians broke it off. Afterward, Crazy Horse reported thirty-six Indians dead. Crook lost nine troopers and one Shoshone scout.

Years later, John Stands in Timber, a descendant of Sitting Bull's followers, was asked why the Indians had withdrawn after fighting so well. He answered simply, "They were tired and hungry, so they went home."[5]

Because the Indians had broken off the fighting, Crook claimed victory. In truth, however, his column had taken a severe beating. Once again, he was forced to withdraw to Fort Fetterman, this time at a critical time in Phil Sheridan's three-column campaign.

Sitting Bull and his followers set up camp in the valley of the Little Bighorn—the river they called the Greasy Grass. On their slow westward trek, their numbers had stayed pretty stable at about 450 lodges. But on the Greasy Grass, reservation Indians began to arrive. In the week following the battle on the Rosebud, their size doubled to about 7,000 people, some 1,800 of them warriors. They celebrated their victory over Three Stars with dancing and feasting.

After clashing with Crook's cavalry at the Rosebud River, the Sioux and Cheyenne moved their camp to the wooded area of the Greasy Grass (Little Bighorn) River shown in the background.

Side-wheeler, shallow-draft steamboats navigated the nation's rivers in the 1800s. *The Expansion*, shown here in the Yellowstone River, is similar to the *Far West* steamer that carried the Seventh Cavalry survivors to safety.

Meanwhile, General Terry met up with Colonel Gibbon on the Yellowstone River at the mouth of the Rosebud on June 21. Neither man knew of Crook's withdrawal from the Rosebud four days earlier. Terry summoned Gibbon, Custer, and other officers for a meeting aboard the Yellowstone steamer *Far West* to map out a strategy for engaging the Indians. Earlier, Major Marcus A. Reno had led a scouting expedition forty-five miles up the Rosebud. Based on his report, the officers concluded that they would find the Indians somewhere along the stream marked Little Bighorn on Terry's map.

Terry's plan called for Custer and the Seventh Cavalry to follow the Indian trail up the Rosebud, cross to the Little Bighorn, and move down its valley from the south. In the meantime, Terry and Gibbon would march up the Yellowstone and

Bighorn to block an Indian escape to the north. This maneuvering would trap Sitting Bull's forces between two columns in a classic pincers movement.

At noon on June 22, the Seventh Cavalry—600-men strong—passed in review to the tune of "Garry Owen" for Terry, Gibbon, and Custer. After the pack train straggled by, Custer, clad in buckskins, shook hands with his fellow officers and wheeled to depart. General Gibbon called after him: "Now Custer, don't be greedy, but wait for us."[6]

"No, I will not,"[7] Custer replied cryptically, and rode off with the Seventh Cavalry.

Gibbon was joking when he told Custer not to be greedy. Everyone understood that whichever column found the Indians first should attack them at once. Everyone expected that the more mobile Custer would very likely be the first to find them. And he did not disappoint expectations.

General John Gibbon was highly respected as a determined and tenacious officer. As a colonel, he led the relief column that arrived too late to save Custer and his command at the Little Bighorn.

Custer with his Indian scouts in camp. Bloody Knife points to a map. The large wall tent was a gift of the Northern Pacific Railroad.

Custer proceeded up the Rosebud and found the Indian trail on June 25, much fresher than had been anticipated. More important, a new trail indicated that the Indians were not in the upper valley of the Little Bighorn, but very close by.

Custer sent his scouts out to locate them. Bloody Knife, an Arikara scout, sighted the huge Indian encampment. He reported its size through an interpreter: "He says we'll find enough Sioux to keep us fighting for two or three days."[8]

Smiling, Custer replied, "I guess we'll get through them in one day."[9]

Sitting Bull was not the only one to experience visions of future happenings at the Little Bighorn. Before Custer led his Seventh Cavalry out of Fort Abraham Lincoln to pursue the nontreaty Indians, all the wives of the officers and enlisted men had been haunted by an inexplicable sense of impending doom.

Annie Yates dreamed that an Indian shot Custer in the head. She was the wife of one of Custer's officers, Company F commander Captain George W. Yates. When Annie told Custer of her dream, he replied, "I cannot die before my time comes, and . . . if by a bullet in the head—Why not?"[10]

And when Lieutenant Francis Gibson's wife learned of his transfer to a company under Custer's immediate command, she felt a "weird something"[11] clutch her soul.

Mark Kellogg, a correspondent for the *Bismarck Tribune* and the *New York Herald,* accompanied the Seventh Cavalry on the Little Bighorn expedition. He reported, "I go with Custer, and I will be in at the death."[12]

En route to the Little Bighorn, "Lonesome Charley" Reynolds, a civilian guide, felt "sure that he was riding to his death."[13]

First Lieutenant Edward S. Godfrey, commander of Company K, sensed that some of the officers seemed "to have a presentiment of their fate."[14] His fellow officer, First Lieutenant George Wallace of Company K, confided to him, "Godfrey, I believe General Custer is going to be killed."[15] Dreams do come true—even death dreams.

Edward S. Godfrey

CHAPTER

FOUR

THE LAST STAND

Soon after discovering the Indian camp, Custer's scouts sighted three separate Lakota war parties nearby. Custer had planned to pause for a day while searching for the Indian village and scouting the terrain. He would then attack on June 26, after Terry and Gibbon had taken up their blocking position. But chances were, at least one of the war parties had spotted his column. If so, he would lose the element of surprise. Worse yet, to Custer's way of thinking, the Indians might scatter as they had many times in the past, and there would be no Indians to fight. A change of plans was needed. Custer decided to attack at once—on June 25, 1876.

Ironically, the three war parties his scouts had sighted were not war parties at all, but rather groups of agency Indians returning to the reservation. Sitting Bull's camp had not been alerted to the Seventh Cavalry's presence.

Custer had not yet seen the Indian encampment himself. He did not know its exact location, and he was unfamiliar with the terrain. Nor was he aware of the size of his Indian opponents. The well-disciplined forces of Sitting Bull, Crazy Horse, and others numbered

Edgar Samuel Paxson's *Battle of Little Bighorn* is one of many artist's renditions of Custer's final moments. Though romanticized, it captures the drama of close mortal combat.

about 1,800 of the finest mounted warriors to be found anywhere. They outnumbered his own forces by a ratio of three to one, more than twice the number the army had expected. By the time he learned the true situation, it would be too late.

At 12:15 PM, forced to devise a strategy as the situation unfolded, Custer led his regiment across the divide between the Rosebud and the Little Bighorn. Still unaware of the superior numbers facing him, he split his command. Custer sent Captain Frederick W. Benteen and three companies (or troops)—125 men in all— to the south. He wanted to make sure the Indians had not wandered into the upper valley of the Little Bighorn.

As Custer continued on a more direct route to the river, he flushed out a party of about forty Lakota warriors. At 2:30 PM, he ordered Major Marcus A. Reno and three troops—175 men—to pursue the Lakotas, cross the river, and attack the village. Custer promised Reno support from the five troops—210 men—he kept under his immediate command. Custer's contingent

Major Marcus A. Reno's questionable decisions at the Little Bighorn created more than a century of controversy over his role in Custer's stunning defeat.

included his brothers, Tom and Boston, his nephew Harry Armstrong "Autie" Reed, and his brother-in-law James Calhoun.

Reno's three troops trotted down the valley toward the village in parallel columns. Custer turned to the north. He probably hoped to strike the northern end of the village while Reno attacked the southern end. When he saw the village for the first time, he sent a message for Benteen to move up immediately.

Meanwhile, once Reno had crossed the river and moved into the valley, he saw dust swirls rising from far ahead. The Indians were not running away but rather were attacking. Reno advanced in columns at a fast trot but quickly shifted into a battle line. Bullets began to whiz all about.

Trooper William Slater recalled his first action well. "I know that for a time I was frightened," he wrote later, "and far more so when I got my first glimpse of the Indians riding about in all directions, firing at us and yelling and whooping like incarnate fiends, all seemingly naked as the day they were born."[1]

The Custer Fight by Charles Marion Russell captures the dash and fervor of an encircling Indian attack.

Faced with hundreds of screaming attackers, Reno halted and ordered his troopers to dismount and form a skirmisher's line. In danger of being overrun, he soon wheeled his line back against the protective stand of timber along the river. Unable to hold position there, Reno re-formed his troops into a column and dashed toward a bluff across the river.

Lakota and Cheyenne warriors swarmed all around them. "As we cut our way through them," Reno wrote later, "the fighting was hand to hand and it was instant death to him who fell from his saddle, or was wounded."[2] He lost thirty-five killed and eleven wounded on the skirmish line. "Lonesome Charley" Reynolds died early in the wild dash for safety. The rest of Reno's troopers dug in under siege on the bluff.

No sooner had the Indians driven the troopers across the river than they discovered more soldiers approaching the other end of their village. Custer had arrived. It was now about 3:30 pm. "I called to my men," Low Dog, an Oglala chief, recalled.

" 'This is a good day to die: follow me.' We massed our men . . . and we rushed right upon them."[3]

The Indians squeezed Custer's two hundred in a pincers movement of their own. A swarm of warriors, mostly Cheyenne under Lame White Man and Hunkpapa led by Gall, crossed the river and attacked Custer from the south. At the same time, Crazy Horse and a mass of Oglalas struck him from the north. Crazy Horse dashed through a narrow gap and singlehandedly cut Custer's right flank in half.

"Crazy Horse was the bravest man I ever saw," recalled Waterman, an Arapaho. "All the soldiers were shooting at him, but he was never hit."[4]

"The Indians kept coming like an increasing flood that could not be checked,"[5] Red Hawk, an Oglala, remembered. Though hopelessly outnumbered, the men of the Seventh Cavalry fought bravely and died like soldiers, as did many of their attackers.

"Once I saw Yellowhair," the Arapaho Left Hand said, referring to Custer. "It was almost at the end of the fight. He was standing up and had pistols in his hands, shooting into the Indians."[6]

Within an hour, the shooting stopped, and Custer and his men—all 210—lay dead on a grassy bluff beside the Little Bighorn. Custer had made his last stand.

The Battle of the Little Bighorn did not end with the annihilation of Custer and the five companies under his immediate command. Four miles up the river, Major Reno and the remnants of his three companies were dug in on the bluff now known as Reno Hill. During his attack and retreat, he had lost 40 dead, 13 wounded, and 17 missing—one half of his command. Only Custer's ill-fated action against the Indian village had saved Reno's troopers from greater losses.

Meanwhile, Captain Benteen had received Custer's message, a note written by the colonel's adjutant, First Lieutenant William W. Cooke: BENTEEN: COME ON. BIG VILLAGE. BE QUICK. BRING PACKS. W. W. COOKE. PS BRING PACS [sic].[7] The message was delivered by Custer's Italian trumpeter John Martin (Giovanni Martini), the last man to see him alive.

Rather than rush to Custer's aid, Benteen instead elected to join forces with Reno. Though both Benteen and Reno had to have heard sounds of heavy gunfire coming from the site of Custer's desperate stand, neither officer offered to join the fighting. Benteen and Reno mounted brief counterattacks, but their Indian attackers soon forced them back to their siege positions on Reno Hill.

The fighting eased after nightfall but resumed at daybreak and continued until about noon. After occasional sniper fire that afternoon, the Indians withdrew at dusk. Benteen described their leaving: "It was in a straight line about three miles long, and I think half a mile wide, as densely packed as animals could be."[8] The siege was over.

Captain Benteen

CHAPTER

FIVE

ECHOES

Sitting Bull and his followers left the Greasy Grass under a screen of billowing smoke from a grass fire they had set to cover their movement. "[A]s dusk approached," noted historians Robert M. Utley and Wilcomb E. Washburn, "a scene took form that the watching soldiers would never forget—a cavalcade of seven thousand Indians, men, women, and children, some mounted, others walking, ponies dragging travois laden with tepees, utensils, and infants, all crawling up the bench across the valley and wending slowly toward the snowy peaks of the Bighorn Mountains."[1] The Indians had learned of General Terry advancing with Colonel Gibbon's column up the north end of the valley.

Terry and Gibbon arrived at the deserted Indian village on the morning of June 27, 1876. Picking through the litter of the hastily abandoned camp, their scouts uncovered grim signs of what had happened. Their findings included "a cavalry saddle, a dead army horse, a bloody and bullet-pierced buckskin shirt marked 'Porter,' gauntlets bearing the inscription 'Yates 7th Cav,' [and] blood-stained underwear."[2]

★ ★ ★ ★ ★ ★ ★ ★ ★ ★ ★ ★ ★ ★ ★ ★ ★

Memorial markers at the Custer Battlefield National Monument stand at the spot where each trooper fell. Custer's marker bears a black shield.

While the rummaging continued, Lieutenant James Bradley rode into camp. He and his mounted infantry detachment had been scouting along the ridges across the river. In a quavering voice, he said to Terry and Gibbon, "I have a very sad report to make. I have counted 197 bodies lying in the hills."[3] They asked if they were white men. He said they all were.

Aghast, General Terry rode on to the bluffs and conveyed the news of Custer's contingent to the tired survivors of the siege at Reno Hill. He ordered Captain Benteen to take his company and bury the dead. The burial party proceeded to what is now Custer Hill. Lieutenant Godfrey described what they found as a "scene of sickening ghastly horror."[4] Most of the bodies had been stripped naked and horribly mutilated. The Sioux and Cheyenne had carried their dead and wounded back down to the village. The number of Indian casualties remains unknown.

Red granite gravestones mark the burial sites of Limber Bones and Closed Hand who fell fighting Custer's Seventh Cavalry at the Little Bighorn River.

This scene was photographed from a Wild West show re-enactment of Custer's Last Stand, a depiction more dramatic than accurate.

They found Custer's body at the northern end of the bluff, beside his blue pendant with white crossed sabers. A cluster of troopers was scattered around him. Unlike most of the others, his body had not been mutilated. He had been shot in the head and in the chest below the heart. Either shot would have been fatal. The body of his brother Tom lay close by, scalped, badly mutilated, and bristling with arrows.

Boston Custer and Autie Reed lay just down the hill from George and Tom. Brother-in-law James Calhoun met his death on an adjacent hill. Near the river lay the body of journalist Mark Kellogg. He had promised to be with Custer "at the death," and he kept his word. In all, 263 officers, men, scouts, and civilians died along the Little Bighorn—210 in Custer's battalion alone. Indian losses remain uncertain but are thought to be about 75 or more, including 10 women and children.

Benteen's burial detail completed their woeful task. "In a great many instances," Sergeant John Ryan confessed, "their arms and legs protruded."[5] The soldiers

marked each shallow grave of their deceased comrades with an inverted cartridge case containing a name and fitted onto a stick.

Late that afternoon, Terry marched his men downstream toward the mouth of the Little Bighorn. They carried the wounded in various hand litters, mule litters, and Indian-style travois and eventually loaded them aboard the waiting river steamer *Far West*.

Controversy over Custer's actions arose as soon as news of the Seventh Cavalry's fate reached the public. Critics condemned him for splitting his command and not waiting for Terry and Gibbon; supporters justified his conduct. General Phil Sheridan noted that if Custer had "waited until his regiment was closed up" the Indians could not have defeated him. "I do not attribute Col. Custer's action to either recklessness or to want of judgement," he went on, "but to misapprehension and a super-abundance of courage."[6]

General Philip H. Sheridan attributed Custer's defeat at the Little Bighorn to "misapprehension and a super-abundance of courage." No officer held Sheridan's confidence to a greater degree than Custer.

As to the courage of Custer and the Seventh Cavalry, General Terry, in a report to General Sheridan, wrote: "There is abundant evidence that a gallant resistance was offered by the troops, but that they were beset on all sides by overpowering numbers."[7] Sitting Bull later affirmed the general's statement, saying, "I tell no lies about dead men. Those men who came with the 'Long Hair' [Custer] were as good men as ever fought."[8]

Custer's wife, Libbie, was devastated when she heard the news. "I wanted to die," she wrote later. "To lose him would be to close the windows of life that let in the sunshine."[9] At her request, Custer's remains were relocated to a final resting place at West Point on the banks of the Hudson. Libbie never remarried and spent the rest of her long life defending her husband's honor and legacy. She died on April 4, 1933, four days before her ninety-first birthday, and was placed beside Custer, her "own bright particular star."[10]

Custer's monument stands next to his grave at the West Point Cemetery. The stone obelisk atop the monument's base replaced a bronze statue of Custer on horseback in 1905, because Libbie Custer didn't like the statue's likeness of her husband.

Sitting Bull, Crazy Horse, and their Cheyenne and Lakota followers won a great victory at the Little Bighorn, but they lost the war. Public outrage over their annihilation of Custer and the Seventh Cavalry prompted Congress to flood the Indian country with additional cavalrymen. And a new commission reached an agreement with agency chiefs to redefine the boundaries of the Sioux reservation so as to exclude the Black Hills.

Additional battles remained to be fought in the Great Sioux War, but time was running out for the Indians and their way of life. In the words of historians Utley and Washburn, "their final defeat lurked unseen in their soaring victory amid the brown hills overlooking the Greasy Grass."[11]

Today, when visitors walk the grassy knolls where Custer and his cavalry made their stand, if they pause and listen, they are apt to hear the echoes of the battle that will not die in the American imagination.

Closed Hand fell while defending the Cheyenne way of life, but the way of life for all Native Americans changed forever a few years later.

Whither do the spirits go? One can only wonder. But anyone who has ever visited a field of battle and heard the whisperings of the past will very likely say there is no better place to find visitors from another dimension. In validation of such speculation, flesh-and-blood visitors to the Little Bighorn Battlefield National Monument have experienced and reported numerous visitors of an unexplained variety.

The Crow people were perhaps the first to recognize the presence of otherworldly others. Their experiences led them to name the park superintendent "ghost herder." They believed when he lowered the flag at sundown, the spirits arose from their graves and walked among them. When he raised the flag in the morning, the spirits returned to their resting places.

Many visitors have reported hearing sounds of Indian warriors galloping through the cemetery on horseback. Another visitor from New Orleans told of having been whisked back in time to witness the battle firsthand. A cab driver from Minneapolis, while driving along Battle Ridge, saw soldiers and warriors engaged in a fight to the death.

One evening in August 1976—a hundred years after the battle—a park ranger visited Last Stand Hill. Alone, he felt a sudden chill come over him and heard the soft murmuring of voices. He did not wait to learn whether they were talking to him.

Several visitors have reported seeing Custer's ghost walking about on Last Stand Hill. Dressed in buckskins, red scarf, and white hat, his yellow hair cut short, he wore a confused expression, they say, as if looking for his brothers. Who can say he was not?

George Custer

1831   Sitting Bull is born somewhere along the Grand River (South Dakota).

1839   Custer is born in New Rumley, Ohio, on December 5.

1861   Custer graduates last in his class at the U.S. Military Academy at West Point.

1868   The Laramie Treaty is signed at Fort Laramie, Dakota Territory, on April 29, guaranteeing ownership of the Black Hills to the Sioux Nation.

1874   Custer leads an expedition into the Black Hills.

1875   President Ulysses S. Grant decides to make war on the nontreaty Indians on November 3.

1876

March 1   General George Crook leads a column of cavalry out of Fort Fetterman, Wyoming, to seek out nontreaty Indians.

March 17   General Crook's column engages nontreaty Indians at the Powder River and is forced to withdraw.

May 17   General Terry moves west out of Fort Abraham Lincoln with a column of troopers, including Custer's Seventh Cavalry, to rendezvous with Colonel Gibbon's column on the Yellowstone River.

May 29   General Crook marches north out of Fort Fetterman again.

Early June   Sitting Bull's followers hold a religious ceremony known as a Sun Dance at their camp on the Rosebud River; Sitting Bull has a vision of soldiers falling into camp.

June 16   Sitting Bull and his followers move their camp to Sun Dance Creek.

June 17   General Crook's column clashes with Lakota and Cheyenne warriors at the Rosebud River; Crook withdraws again to Fort Fetterman.

June 21   General Terry meets with Colonel Gibbon on the Yellowstone River at the mouth of the Rosebud.

June 22   The Seventh Cavalry passes in review and heads up the Rosebud to search for Sitting Bull's camp.

June 25   Custer's scouts discover Sitting Bull's camp on the Little Bighorn; Custer decides to attack:

    12:15 P.M.   Custer improvises attack plan as the situation unfolds.

    2:30 P.M.   Custer orders Reno to attack the village; Reno attacks and withdraws to Reno Hill.

    3:30 P.M.   Custer arrives at the north end of the village; Indians engage him at once.

    4:30 P.M.   Custer and his men are all killed; the Indians put the combined forces of Reno and Benteen under siege.

June 26   Indians leave the Little Bighorn; siege ends.

June 27   Terry and Gibbon arrive at the Little Bighorn, bury the dead, and transport the wounded to the river steamer *Far West* on the Yellowstone.

1890   Sitting Bull is shot dead by Lakota police at the Standing Rock Indian Agency.

1933   Libbie Custer dies and is laid to rest next to her husband at West Point.

1980   Mardell Plainfeather sees a vision of two Indian warriors sitting on their horses at the Custer Battlefield National Monument.

Chapter 1 "We Shall Fight as Brave Men Fight"

1. Bob Reece, "Visitors of Another Kind." http://www.friendslittlebighorn.com/ghosts-along-the-little-bighorn.htm, p. 2.

2. Ibid.

3. Robert M. Utley, *Cavalier in Buckskin: George Armstrong Custer and the Western Military Frontier* (Norman: University of Oklahoma Press, 1988), p. 167.

4. Nathaniel Philbrick, *The Last Stand: Custer, Sitting Bull, and the Battle of the Little Bighorn* (New York: Penguin Books, 2011), p. 20.

5. D. A. Kinsley, *Custer: Favor the Bold, A Soldier's Story* (New York: Promontory Press, 1992), p. 468.

6. Ibid.

7. Jeffrey D. Wert, *Custer: The Controversial Life of George Armstrong Custer.* (New York: Simon & Schuster, 1996), p. 358.

Chapter 2 Soldiers Falling into Camp

1. John S. Gray, *Centennial Campaign: The Sioux War of 1876.* Norman: University of Oklahoma Press, 1988, p. 31.

2. Wayne Michael Sarf, *The Little Bighorn Campaign, March–September 1876.* Great Campaigns Series (Conshohocken, PA: Combined Books, 1993), p. 30.

3. Nathaniel Philbrick, *The Last Stand: Custer, Sitting Bull, and the Battle of the Little Bighorn* (New York: Penguin Books, 2011), p. 54.

4. James Welch, with Paul Stekler, *Killing Custer: The Battle of the Little Bighorn and the Fate of the Plains Indians* (New York: W. W. Norton & Company, 1994), p. 51.

5. Jeffrey D. Wert, *Custer: The Controversial Life of George Armstrong Custer* (New York: Simon & Schuster, 1996), p. 301.

Chapter 3 Great Expectations

1. Robert Kammen, Joe Marshall, and Frederick Lefthand, *Soldiers Falling into Camp: The Battles at the Rosebud and the Little Bighorn* (Encampment, WY: Affiliated Writers of America/Publishers, 1992), p. 3.

2. Ibid., p. 6.

3. Nathaniel Philbrick, *The Last Stand: Custer, Sitting Bull, and the Battle of the Little Bighorn* (New York: Penguin Books, 2011), p. 93.

4. Ibid.

5. Wayne Michael Sarf, *The Little Bighorn Campaign, March–September 1876.* Great Campaigns Series (Conshohocken, PA: Combined Books, 1993), p. 113.

6. Jeffrey D. Wert, *Custer: The Controversial Life of George Armstrong Custer* (New York: Simon & Schuster, 1996), p. 336.

7. Ibid.

8. Robert M. Utley, *Cavalier in Buckskin: George Armstrong Custer and the Western Military Frontier* (Norman: University of Oklahoma Press, 1988), p. 181.

9. Ibid.

10. Philbrick, p. 18.

11. Ibid.

12. D. A. Kinsley, *Custer: Favor the Bold, A Soldier's Story* (New York: Promontory Press, 1992), p. 516.

13. Sarf, p. 159.

14. Ibid.

15. Ibid., p. 175.

Chapter 4 The Last Stand

1. Bruce A. Rosenberg, *Custer and the Epic of Defeat* (University Park: The Pennsylvania State University Press, 1974), p. 33.

2. Ibid., p. 37.

3. Robert M. Utley and Wilcomb E. Washburn, *The American Heritage History of the Indian Wars.* Edited by Anne Moffat and Richard F. Snow (New York: Barnes & Noble Books, 1992) p. 273.

4. Nathaniel Philbrick, *The Last Stand: Custer, Sitting Bull, and the Battle of the Little Bighorn* (New York: Penguin Books, 2011), p. 268.

5. Ibid., p. 269.

6. D. A. Kinsley, *Custer: Favor the Bold, A Soldier's Story* (New York: Promontory Press, 1992), p. 534.

7. Wayne Michael Sarf, *The Little Bighorn Campaign, March–September 1876.* Great Campaigns Series (Conshohocken, PA: Combined Books, 1993), p. 213.

8. Ibid., p. 244.

Chapter 5 Echoes

1. Robert M. Utley and Wilcomb E. Washburn. *The American Heritage History of the Indian Wars.* Edited by Anne Moffat and Richard F. Snow (New York: Barnes & Noble Books, 1992) p. 276.

2. Ibid.

3. Edgar I. Stewart, *Custer's Luck* (Norman: University of Oklahoma Press, 1955), p. 466.

4. Robert M. Utley, *Cavalier in Buckskin: George Armstrong Custer and the Western Military Frontier* (Norman: University of Oklahoma Press, 1988), p. 192.

5. Wayne Michael Sarf, *The Little Bighorn Campaign, March–September 1876.* Great Campaigns Series (Conshohocken, PA: Combined Books, 1993), p. 262.

6. Ibid., p. 265.

7. Charles M. Robinson III, *A Good year to Die: The Story of the Great Sioux War* (New York: Random House, 1995), p. 211.

8. Stewart, p. 459.

9. Jeffrey D. Wert, *Custer: The Controversial Life of George Armstrong Custer* (New York: Simon & Schuster, 1996), p. 356.

10. Ibid., p. 357.

11. Utley and Washburn, p. 276.

Books

Gary, Jeffrey. *The Battle of the Little Bighorn*. Graphic History of the American West Series. Gareth Stevens Publishing, 2012.

Goble, Paul. *Custer's Last Battle: Red Hawk's Account of the Battle of the Little Bighorn*. Bloomington, IN: Wisdom Tales, 2013.

King, Zelda. *The Battle of the Little Bighorn: Both Sides of the Story*. New York: Rosen Publishing Group, 2009.

Uschan, Michael V. *The Battle of the Little Bighorn*. Landmark Events in American History Series. New York: Gareth Stevens Publishing, 2002.

Works Consulted

Axelrod, Alan. *Chronicle of the Indian Wars: From Colonial Times to Wounded Knee*. New York: Prentice Hall General Reference, 1993.

Barnett, Louise. *Touched by Fire: The Life, Death, and Mythic Afterlife of George Armstrong Custer*. New York: Henry Holt and Company, 1996.

Brady, Cyrus Townshend. *The Sioux Indian Wars: From the Powder River to the Little Big Horn*. New York: Indian Head Books, 1992.

Brininstool, E. A. *Troopers with Custer: Historic Incidents of the Battle of the Little Big Horn*. Mechanicsburg, PA: Stackpole Books, 1994.

Carroll, John M., ed. *They Rode with Custer: A Biographical Directory of the Men that Rode with General George A. Custer*. Mattituck, NY: J. M. Carroll & Company, 1993.

Chamberlain, Keith. *Ghosts of the Little Bighorn*. Tullibody, Scotland, UK: Diadem Books, 2011.

Connell, Evan S. *Son of the Morning Star*. New York: Promontory Press, 1993.

Custer, George Armstrong. *My Life on the Plains*. New York: Carol Publishing Group, 1990.

Fox, Richard Allan, Jr. *Archaeology, History, and Custer's Last Battle: The Little Big Horn Reexamined*. Norman: University of Oklahoma Press, 1993.

Graham, W. A. *The Story of the Little Big Horn: Custer's Last Fight*. Mechanicsburg, PA: Stackpole Books, 1994.

Gray, John S. *Custer's Last Campaign: Mitch Boyer and the Little Bighorn Reconstructed*. Lincoln: University of Nebraska Press, 1991.

———. *Centennial Campaign: The Sioux War of 1876*. Norman: University of Oklahoma Press, 1988.

Greene, Jerome A., ed. *Lakota and Cheyenne: Indian Views of the Great Sioux War, 1876–1877*. Norman: University of Oklahoma Press, 1994.

Hutton, Paul Andrew ed. *The Custer Reader*. Lincoln: University of Nebraska Press, 1992.

———. *Soldiers West: Biographies from the Military Frontier*. Lincoln: University of Nebraska Press, 1987.

Kammen, Robert, Joe Marshall, and Frederick Lefthand. *Soldiers Falling into Camp: The Battles at the Rosebud and the Little Bighorn*. Encampment, WY: Affiliated Writers of America, 1992.

Kinsley, D. A. *Custer: Favor the Bold, A Soldier's Story*. New York: Promontory Press, 1992.

Kuhlman, Charles. *Legend into History and Did Custer Disobey Orders at the Battle of the Little Big Horn?* Mechanicsburg, PA: Stackpole Books, 1994.

Merington, Marguerite. *The Custer Story: The Life and Letters of General George A. Custer and His Wife Elizabeth*. New York: Barnes & Noble, 1994.

Miller, David Humphreys. *Custer's Fall: The Native American Side of the Story*. New York: Meridian, 1992.

Philbrick, Nathaniel. *The Last Stand: Custer, Sitting Bull, and the Battle of the Little Bighorn*. New York: Penguin Books, 2011.

Robinson, Charles M., III. *A Good Year to Die: The Story of the Great Sioux War*. New York: Random House, 1995.

Rosenberg, Bruce A. *Custer and the Epic of Defeat*. University Park: The Pennsylvania State University Press, 1974.

Sarf, Wayne Michael. *The Little Bighorn Campaign, March–September 1876*. Great Campaigns Series. Conshohocken, PA: Combined Books, 1993.

Stewart, Edgar I. *Custer's Luck*. Norman: University of Oklahoma Press, 1955.

Utley, Robert M. *Cavalier in Buckskin: George Armstrong Custer and the Western Military Frontier*. Norman: University of Oklahoma Press, 1988.

——, Robert M., and Wilcomb E. Washburn. *The American Heritage History of the Indian Wars*. New York: Barnes & Noble Books, 1992.

Welch, James, with Paul Stekler. *Killing Custer: The Battle of the Little Bighorn and the Fate of the Plains Indians*. New York: W. W. Norton & Company, 1994.

Wert, Jeffrey D. *Custer: The Controversial Life of George Armstrong Custer*. New York: Simon & Schuster, 1996.

On the Internet

Eyewitness to History. "The Battle of the Little Bighorn, 1876."
http://www.eyewitnesstohistory.com/pfcuster.htm

Haunted Houses. "Little Bighorn Hauntings. Little Bighorn Battlefield."
http://hauntedhouses.com/states/mt/little_bighorn.htm

Lewis, Fairweather. "Ghosts of the Little Bighorn."
http://fairweatherlewis.wordpress.com/2011/06/25/ghosts-of-the-little-bighorn/

Powers, Thomas. "How the Battle of Little Bighorn Was Won."
http://www.smithsonianmag.com/history-archaeology/How-the-Battle-of-Little-Bighorn-Was-Won.html

Reece, Bob. "Visitors of Another Kind."
http://www.friendslittlebighorn.com/ghosts-along-the-little-bighorn.hto

besiege (bee-SEEJ)—To lay siege; to gather around an enemy's fort, city, or other shelter in order to prevent messengers from leaving and supplies from arriving.

brevet (brih-VET)—A military rank higher than the one for which the officer is paid.

column (KOL-um)—A long, narrow formation of troops, whether on foot, mounted, or in vehicles.

contingent (kon-TIN-jent)—A group of troops that come from one place and form part of a larger force.

convergence (kon-VERJ-ents)—A coming together at the same point.

encampment (en-KAMP-ment)—A camp.

otherworldly (oth-er-WURLD-lee)—Concerned more with a spiritual or imagined world than the real world.

pincers movement (PIN-serz MOOV-ment)—An attack in which forces converge from opposite sides on an enemy position.

predetermine (pree-dih-TUR-min)—To decide something in advance.

rendezvous (RAHN-day-voo)—A prearranged meeting or meeting place.

strategy (STRAT-eh-jee)—The planning and directing of the whole operation of a campaign or war.

supernatural (soo-per-NAT-chuh-rul)—Of or caused by a power above the forces of nature.

trance (trants)—A sleeplike state, as that induced by hypnosis.

travois (trah-VWAH)—A simple sled used by Plains Indians, usually pulled by a horse, made of two trailing poles with a platform in the middle for the cargo.

unceded (un-SEED-ed)—Not yielded or granted, typically by treaty.